# CRETE
## ISLAND
## OF MYSTERY

ILLUSTRATED BY W. T. MARS

# CRETE:
## ISLAND
## OF MYSTERY

## BY LEONARD COTTRELL

PRENTICE-HALL, INC. ENGLEWOOD CLIFFS, N. J.

To FIONA
hoping she will visit Crete
when she is older.

# CONTENTS

# ONE

# THE LEGEND OF CRETE

> Out in the dark blue sea there lies a land called
> Crete, a rich and lovely land, washed by the waves
> on every side, densely peopled and boasting ninety
> cities . . . One of the ninety towns is a great city
> called Knossos, and there, for nine years, King
> Minos ruled and enjoyed the friendship of almighty
> Zeus.

So wrote the ancient Greek poet Homer in his famous
epic poem *The Odyssey,* which describes the wander-
ings of the heroes of the Trojan War in their efforts to
get back to their homeland of Greece.

Crete is a long, narrow, mountainous island lying out
in the Mediterranean Sea, roughly midway between the
Greek mainland, Asia and Egypt. According to Homer
and other, later, Greek writers, Crete was ruled by King
Minos and his three sons, long before the time of the
Trojan War, when the Cretan king, Idomeneus, and his
famous archers fought at Troy. Poets are not always
reliable historians, but a later Greek writer, and very
great historian, Thucydides, confirmed that a King

Minos ruled not only Crete but the surrounding islands, and that he "put down piracy." But just *when* King Minos ruled, or whether there were in fact many kings of that name (as there were many Pharaohs of Egypt) no one knew.

There were, however, fascinating legends, of which the most famous is the one concerning the Thread of Ariadne. Minos, it is said, had once conquered Athens and as tribute he demanded that each year seven noble Athenian youths and seven maidens be sent to his capital city, Knossos, there to be sacrificed to the *Minotaur*. This was a monster, half bull and half man, which Minos kept in the innermost part of a *Labyrinth*, or maze of corridors, which the smith Daedalus had built for the King under his palace.

Many young Athenians perished in this way until one year Theseus, son and heir of Aegeus, King of Athens, volunteered to go to Crete as one of the seven youths. Minos' daughter, the lovely Ariadne, fell in love with the handsome Athenian prince. One day she gave him a large ball of thread saying, "When you enter the Labyrinth, fasten one end of the thread near the entrance and unwind it as you go. Then, if you succeed in slaying the Minotaur, you will be able to find your way out again by following the thread."

Theseus boldly entered the grim, dark corridors, hearing in the distance the fearsome bellowing of the bull-monster. Although he carried no weapon, he slew the Minotaur "by smiting him with his fists," as one Greek writer puts it. Then, following Ariadne's thread, he found his way out again. He managed to escape from Crete, taking Ariadne with him. And that was the end

8

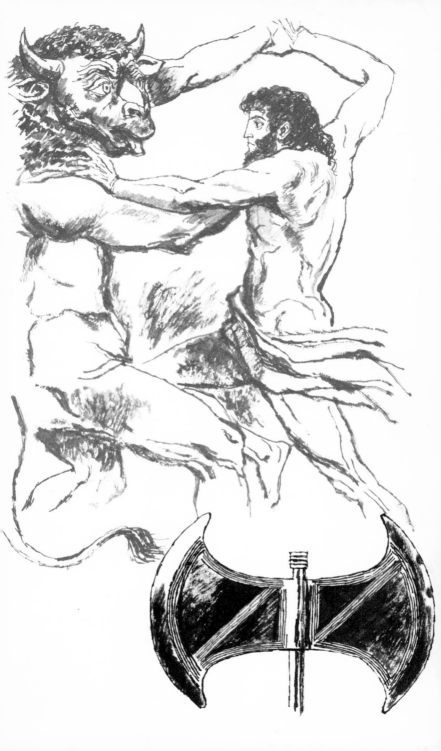

of the bull-monster and the yearly tribute from Athens. Or so says one version of the tale.

Was the story of Theseus and the Minotaur merely a legend, or could this, and other legends of Crete perhaps have been based on historical truth? Before we try to answer that, let us look for a moment at the true story of a man who believed in legends—a man called Heinrich Schliemann.

# TWO

# SCHLIEMANN
# THE TREASURE-HUNTER

*Archaeology* began as treasure-hunting. Once it became known that the peoples of the ancient world were accustomed to burying their kings, queens, princes and princesses accompanied by rich and beautiful offerings, ruthless and daring men made it their job to loot the tombs. We know that this happened in Ancient Egypt more than three thousand years ago. It also took place in Mesopotamia, China, Mexico, South America and other places. As a result, many beautiful things have been lost to the world. Much of the gold and silver was melted down and sold.

Very much later, about two hundred years ago, scholars and collectors began to prize this buried treasure not merely for its value in terms of cash, but for its beauty and rarity. Thus it happened that private collections and great national museums acquired lovely and precious objects, such as the golden crowns and ornaments of Ancient Egyptian kings and queens, the sculpture and painting which had adorned their palaces, the gold-inlaid bronze weapons which had lain beside them in their graves. Rich private collectors and the agents of museums dug, or employed men to dig, in Egypt, Mesopotamia, Greece, Italy and Western Europe, the Far East, Central and South America. Many rare, rich and beautiful things were found.

Nevertheless, these men were still mainly treasure-hunters, and a true archaeologist is not a treasure-hunter. The archaeologist is looking mainly for *facts,* and the objects he finds, whether they happen to be gold-encased chariots, jewelry, or simple scraps of pottery, are of value to him only insofar as they tell him something about the lives, the thoughts and the ideas of the long-dead people whose buried tombs or cities he is investigating.

The true archaeologist is a kind of explorer. Just as the explorer reveals to the world rivers, mountains, forests and unknown tribes which it did not know existed, so the archaeologist re-creates the lives and customs of peoples who lived thousands of years before we were born. But though all this began with treasure-hunting, there have been men who *began* by looking for gold and precious things, but who later became more interested in the people who had made and buried those things. Such a man was Heinrich Schliemann, who was born in 1822 at Neu Buckow, in Germany.

As a ten-year-old boy, Heinrich Schliemann was fascinated by the stories of the war between the Greeks and Trojans described in the works of Homer (who was born more than 2,500 years before Schliemann's time). At the period when Schliemann grew to manhood, most scholars believed that Troy was an imaginary city, that in fact the whole story of the Trojan War was a fable.

Mask of Agamemnon (Mycenae)

But Heinrich, who from his earliest years had wanted to dig for treasure, firmly believed that Troy had existed. He had determined that, when he grew up and made enough money, he would travel to the coast of Turkey—the legendary site of Troy—and dig until he found it.

Although he had little education, Schliemann was an extremely clever young man. Before he was thirty, he had made a vast fortune as an indigo merchant, learned thirteen languages, and traveled widely, including several visits to the United States. Then, at the age of forty-nine, he gave up business and devoted all of his time to archaeology. In Athens, he met and fell in love with a beautiful Greek girl named Sophia Engastromenos. She was only sixteen, but she returned his love. They married, sailed to Turkey, and began digging under a great mound called *Hissarlik*.

Then Schliemann triumphed over the learned men who had scoffed at him. For there *was* a buried city there, indeed, several buried cities, one above the other. One of them, surely, must be the city of King Priam which Homer had described. But which? Schliemann had no means of knowing, but he and his one hundred and fifty workmen dug on for three years, shifting 250,-000 cubic meters of debris and laying bare a succession of mighty walls.

During this long time, in which he and Sophia worked in intense cold and parching heat, Schliemann, who had begun mainly as a treasure-hunter, became an archaeologist. He made drawings and plans not only of the buildings, but of all the things he found, such as pottery and tools of a type never seen before. He pub-

14

lished the result of his work in a great book called *Ilios*, which makes fascinating reading. And in the end, on the very day before he had decided to give up his work, he was rewarded by finding treasure.

That day he noticed something bright and metallic gleaming in a crevice of a wall. Always quick-witted, he told Sophia, "Call the *paidos* [rest-period]. Tell the workmen it is my birthday and they can have the afternoon off with full wages." The Turkish workmen trooped away and then the two excavators, like excited children, carried their finds up to a wooden hut which Schliemann had built on top of the mound. There were lovely golden diadems obviously intended for a woman, vessels of gold, silver and bronze, golden plaques intended for sewing on dresses, golden goblets, rings, and much fine pottery, again of a kind hitherto unknown. Heinrich was now certain he had found the treasure of Priam, King of Troy, and that the wonderful diadems, one of which contained 16,353 separate golden pieces, had belonged to the most beautiful woman of the time, Helen of Troy. In his book he tells us how he lifted the diadem and placed it on the dark hair of his young wife.

# THREE

## SCHLIEMANN FOLLOWS MORE LEGENDS

Now Heinrich again turned his attention to his beloved Homer. In his other great poem, the *Iliad*, which describes the actual events of the Trojan War, Homer had mentioned a powerful chieftain called Agamemnon, who had fought in that war. According to Homer, Agamemnon was lord of a great citadel called Mycenae, which overlooked the Plain of Argos, in Greece. It was Agamemnon who had led the Greek hosts to Troy and the legends stated that on his return to Mycenae he was murdered by his wife.

Sixteen hundred years before Schliemann's time, a Greek traveler named Pausanias had visited Mycenae, which even then was a ruin, and said that he had seen the gravestones above the tombs of Agamemnon and his followers, and also those of Agamemnon's wicked wife, Clytemnestra, and her fellow traitors.

So, following the clue left by Pausanias, Heinrich and Sophia went to Greece, to Mycenae, dug within the walls of the Citadel, and were again rewarded by treasure. It was even more splendid than that of Troy.

16

At the bottom of deep shafts cut out of the rocky soil lay the bodies of nineteen people—men, women and two small children. Golden masks lay on the faces of the men, and on their chests were breastplates of gold. The bodies of the two children were wrapped in sheet gold. Beside the men lay their swords, daggers and drinking cups of gold and silver. The women had their boxes for toiletries. Their long-skirted dresses, which had, of course, decayed, had been ornamented with hundreds of golden plaques in the shapes of bees, cuttle-fish and spirals.

Nothing like this had ever been found before on the mainland of Greece. The objects were quite unlike the well-known Greek art with which we are familiar. The dress of the women, the weapons of the men, inlaid with vigorous scenes of hunting and warfare, the shapes of the gold and silver cups—all were unique at that time. They were not Classical Greek. They were not Egyptian. They were not Oriental. Schliemann, of course, believed that they were the treasures of Agamemnon and his fellow-princes and princesses, and that they dated from the Trojan War which at that time was thought to have been fought in about 1180 B.C. But more cautious scholars were content to call them "Mycenaean," after the place where Schliemann found them.

After his triumphs at Troy and Mycenae, Schliemann became famous. He was feted in England, became a friend of the Prime Minister, William Gladstone, and lectured to many distinguished audiences. He returned to Greece determined to investigate other sites described by Homer. He excavated another powerful Mycenaean city called Tiryns, also mentioned by Homer, situated near the sea not far from Mycenae. It can still be seen in all its glory, even to the galleries of stone, with slits through which the archers fired. He employed more experienced excavators to help him, and these men sometimes cast doubts on Heinrich's belief that the cities he had explored dated from the Trojan War, believing them to be of earlier date. However, nothing would shake the great German excavator's faith, and when he died, in the year 1890, it still remained firm.

Why was he so certain? Well, Homer had described Troy, and there *was* a Troy. Homer had written of "Mycenae, rich in gold," and Schliemann had found the gold. But there was more to it than that. To take just a few examples: In Homer's description of the fight between Achilles and Hector, both warriors carried great body-shields of leather which protected them from neck to ankle. Such shields were depicted on Mycenaean daggers, and they were quite unlike the typical round Greek shields of what we call Classical times (roughly between 700-300 B.C.).

Again, there is the well-known description in Homer of the cup owned by the old warrior, Nestor, which was of gold with ornaments depicting two birds feeding. Such a cup was found at Mycenae, though it was much smaller than Nestor's. Perhaps more interesting than these examples, however, is the fact that the buildings themselves, at Mycenae, Tiryns and Troy, are so like those described by Homer. The central feature of each fortified city is the *megaron*, or great hall, with a round fireplace in the center surrounded by pillars. Such buildings are described by Homer. Agamemnon lived

18

in such a megaron. So did his brother, Menelaus, husband of Helen, and so did the "wily Odysseus" in his island home of Ithaka.

# FOUR

## THE MYSTERY
## OF THE "MILK-STONES"

After his successes at Troy, Mycenae and Tiryns, what could be more natural than that Schliemann should turn his attention to another site mentioned by Homer—*Knossos* in Crete? Knossos, as we saw at the beginning of this book, was the legendary home of King Minos, and the setting for the story of "Theseus and the Minotaur." Accordingly, some years before he died Schliemann went to Crete, determined to dig at Knossos. He attempted to buy land at Knossos, but when the Cretan who owned the land tried to cheat him, he called off the purchase. How near he was to yet another great discovery we shall soon see.

The turns and twists of our story are almost as involved as the Labyrinth itself, so, like Theseus, we have to keep a firm hold on the thread which, like the successive clues in a detective story, will eventually lead us to the truth. Incidentally, the old Greek word for *thread* was *kliuwa*, which means *clue* in English.

So, with this in mind, before we follow in the path of Sir Arthur Evans, the great English archaeologist whose excavations succeeded those of Schliemann, let us look at a few more Cretan legends.

It was said that the real father of Theseus was not Aegeus but the sea-god, *Poseidon,* who was sometimes called "the Earth-Shaker." Homer said of him, "In Bulls does the Earth-Shaker delight." Clue Number One. Clue Number Two: Minos employed a great engineer-architect named Daedalus to build his palace at Knossos. Clue Number Three: When Zeus, the King of all the Gods, fell in love with the daughter of King Agenor of Tyre, as she was playing with her maidens by the sea-shore, he disguised himself as a fine bull. One would have thought this would have alarmed the girl, but not at all. She went up to the animal to fondle it, where-upon Zeus quickly got her on his back and swam with her, out to sea. And where did he take her? To Crete. She was called *Europa.* Europa, the word from which the whole continent of Europe takes its name.

Remembering these clues then, let us return to the story of Sir Arthur Evans and his excavations at Knossos.

When Sir Arthur Evans first went to Crete, the site of the ancient city of Knossos was well known, although it had never been properly excavated. Knossos lies in a valley, at a point near the north coast of Crete a few miles from the modern port of Herakleion.

If this were an invented story, you would expect that Sir Arthur Evans would have explored Crete because of its legends, just as Heinrich Schliemann had been led by his belief in Homer to discover Troy and My-cenae. But this is a true story, and life has a way of being much more complicated than any novel. The fact is that Sir Arthur Evans, who had met and admired

Schliemann, did not believe that the Mycenaean remains discovered by the German archaeologist belonged to the period of the Trojan War. He suspected that they were older, but could not prove it.

Although they were both rich men of strong personality, Schliemann and Evans were unlike in almost every other respect. Schliemann was the son of a poor parson and had received little education. Sir Arthur was a scholar from a family of scholars. Moreover, he did not make his fortune, but inherited it. After a distinguished career at Oxford University, Evans traveled widely in eastern Europe, and became for a time a war correspondent. He once got a valuable news story from a rebel leader by first swimming a fast-running river, naked except for his hat, in which he had put his notebook!

He loved riding and swimming, was tough and resourceful, and had a strong will. But at the same time he was a man of learning, and loved nothing more than to wander in search of Greek and Roman remains in the Balkan country which we now call Yugoslavia. When Schliemann made his historic discoveries it seemed to Evans, as to other men, that there must once have existed, in Europe, a rich civilization, far older than those of Greece or Rome, but which had disappeared and been forgotten. The lovely objects found by Schliemann—the rich art, the fine buildings—proved this. But if these people, whom Schliemann called the Mycenaeans, were so civilized, surely they must have had a writing system, like the ancient Egyptians, the Assyrians and the Babylonians. Yet not one trace of any writing had been found.

This puzzle kept worrying Evans' acute, scholarly mind. At the time when, as a young man, he first began studying the ancient remains of Greece and the Balkan countries, he certainly was not particularly interested in ancient legends. What he was looking for was some clue to the writing system which may have been used by the Mycenaeans, or perhaps even before the Mycenaeans. And one day, when he and his friend John (later Sir John) Myres, were rooting about among the trays of the antique dealers in a back street in Athens, he stumbled on a clue.

On one of the trays Evans came upon a number of tiny little cylinders of glazed clay, each hardly bigger than his thumbnail. He was very near-sighted, but if he held a small object, such as a coin, close to his eye he could see it with almost microscopic accuracy. He turned excitedly to his friend and said, "John, look at this."

Myres looked closely. "I can see some tiny marks on it," he commented. Evans took the tiny object back and re-examined it. "I think those marks are some kind of writing," he said, then asked the dealer, "Where did you get these things?"

"From Crete, sir," answered the dealer, "from Crete . . ."

With Myres, Evans went to Crete and immediately fell in love with the island. He liked the mountains and the hardy Cretan mountaineers. They were tough, lithe, dark men who reminded him of the fierce fighters of the Balkans. He liked the remoteness of the island, its magical atmosphere of high, snow-covered peaks, overlooking gentle valleys and grassy plains. And then

Tablet with Script (Knossos, Crete)

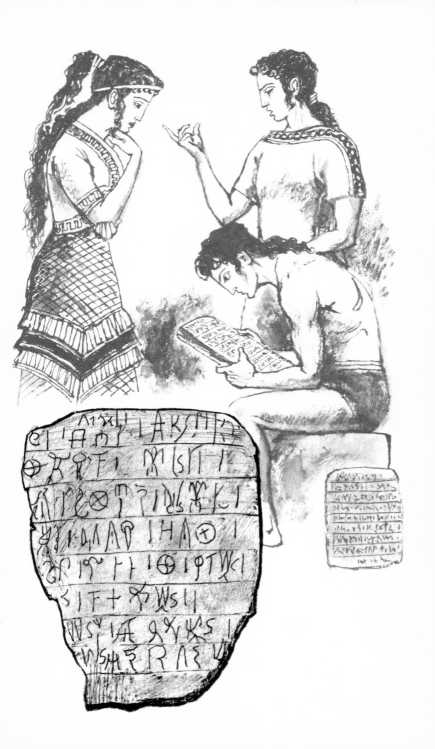

the legends began to speak softly to him—of Zeus, king of the Gods, who was said to have been born on Mount Ida, in Crete; of King Minos, of Theseus and Ariadne.

The two friends journeyed on horseback throughout the island, finding many more examples of the strange little cylinders, each of which had a hole bored through the center as if for hanging around the neck or wrist. The Cretans called them "milk-stones". Their women-folk wore them as charms when they were nursing their babies. But Evans recognized that they were in fact "bead-seals" and were very ancient. They reminded him of similar seals which the ancient Babylonians used some 4,000 years ago. Those Babylonian seals were used to seal documents, and the Cretan examples also seemed to have signs on them—and not only signs, but pictures.

Evans determined to return to Crete as soon as possible, to buy land at Knossos, and to dig there. Even then he was not looking for underground cities or palaces. All he hoped to find were tablets of baked clay —such as the Babylonians had also used—perhaps bearing the ancient Cretan script or writing system which he was certain must once have existed.

# FIVE

# A BURIED PALACE

By 1899, Evans had secured a plot of land at Knossos, and in that year he returned to the island, accompanied by two archaeologists, D. G. Hogarth, who had distinguished himself in Syrian excavations, and Duncan Mackenzie, a painstaking excavator who was noted for the care and skill with which he kept records of archaeological "digs."

Their arrival was signalled by one of the most violent thunderstorms within living memory. Lightning flashed from the peak of Mount Ida, as if Zeus himself were marking the occasion. This may sound fanciful, but it is a curious fact that, again and again during Evans' career as an archaeologist, events occurred which seemed for a moment to put him into direct contact with the long-dead people whose world he was to rediscover, with their Gods and their religious beliefs.

There is nothing spectacular about the site of Knossos. It does not stand on a high, rocky hill, like Mycenae. There is just a low, flat-topped mound, roughly rectangular in shape, with a shallow ravine bordering it on one side. Beyond it, to the south, a broad valley ascends into the mountains.

Evans had selected this site, first, because of its historical associations with Minos, and second, because a few years earlier a Cretan gentleman, appropriately bearing the same name—Minos—had made a few trenches and discovered some buried walls and a number of huge clay jars called, in Greek, *pithoi*. Evans recruited Cretan workmen and began digging. Almost at once great walls came to light—long, narrow chambers which had evidently been storage rooms. Within some of them stood jars, high enough to hide a man as Ali Baba hid in the Tales of the Arabian Nights. But these huge jugs had evidently contained olive oil and other products of the island. The excavators also noticed that at some remote date there had been a great fire. Soot from the burning oil still stained the white stone walls.

Each long storeroom, or *magazine,* had strange rectangular pits, in some of which Evans found minute fragments of gold leaf. He believed that these may have been "safe deposits" which could once have held valuable golden objects like those found by Schliemann at Mycenae. The type of pottery he found, and the general style of the architecture, immediately recalled the "Mycenaean" objects found by the German archaeologist —and at first Evans thought he had found yet another Mycenaean building. But as he and his colleagues dug deeper and deeper, they changed their minds. Evans wrote in his diary for the year 1899: ". . . the great period goes at least well back to *pre*-Mycenaean times."

Within a very short time, Evans discovered what he had been seeking. In rooms adjoining the storerooms, he came upon large numbers of baked-clay tablets, each inscribed with an unknown form of writing akin to the tiny "squiggles" he had observed on the bead-seals. In fact, he found on these tablets two forms of writing which he called "Linear A" and "Linear B." Although he studied them throughout the rest of his long life, he never succeeded in deciphering these mysterious languages, but he found something unexpected and much more exciting—the massive remains of a superb palace, of which the storerooms were only a small part. As month followed month, Evans and his helpers were amazed by the size and complexity of the great building which lay hidden beneath the mound.

There were courtyards and corridors; a maze of rooms, all at different levels. There were staircases of smooth, polished stone. There were the remains of tapering wooden columns which had supported the roof. There was an elaborate system of drainage, with water channels and earthenware pipes laid deep underground. Indeed, the whole building appeared, with its underground rooms and corridors to have been built over a labyrinth. Naturally, Evans' thoughts turned to the legend of King Minos and his engineer-architect, Daedalus, who had built the Cretan Labyrinth.

Day by day, and month by month, more and more wonders were revealed to Evans and his excavators. On the walls were beautiful colored *frescoes*, or paintings, depicting slim young men with curled hair, and women in tight-waisted, flounced dresses, with elaborately dressed hair, piled and curled on top of their heads, and with flowing ringlets falling onto their shoulders.

Then came the most dramatic discovery of all: *the*

*throne room*. First there was an anteroom opening onto a central court. Then, beyond that, a room with seats on three sides of it, overlooking a rectangular pit, with steps leading down into it. At first Evans thought this was a bath, until he discovered there was no outlet for waste water. This pit, Evans later concluded, must have had some kind of religious significance. Beyond the north wall of this inner chamber stood the throne itself. It was made of gypsum, and had a high back, and was raised on a square base. There, in its original position stood—and still stands—the throne of King Minos, the oldest throne in Europe by two thousand years.

Then more and more beautiful frescoes came to light: one showing olive sprays in flower; another of a boy gathering saffron; one of people walking in a solemn procession, another of a great charging bull.

Now, like Schliemann, Evans began to study the ancient legends more closely. Who had built this Palace? Who had lived in it? What kind of people were they? And at what period of time had they lived? Soon he found the answers to some of these questions. The slim-waisted, dark young men depicted on the frescoes were similar to those represented on certain Egyptian tombs dating from about 1550 B.C. But the people shown in these pictures painted on the walls of Egyptian tombs were not Egyptians, but visitors to Egypt, whom the Egyptians called the "Keftiu," who came, they said, "from the Isles of the Great Green Sea" (the Mediterranean).

Here, shown in color on the walls of the Knossian Palace, were the mysterious "Keftiu" whom the Egyptians had known 3,000 years ago. And there was some-

Golden Pendant (Crete)

thing else, even more astonishing: As well as the fresco of the charging bull, which Evans found on the walls of the north portico of the Palace, in another part of the Palace he found another picture of a bull. But this time there were three human figures as well. One, a young man, was somersaulting over the back of the animal. A second, evidently a girl athlete, was grasping one of its horns, while a third girl was standing on tiptoe with upraised arms, as if to catch the young male athlete as he finished his leap.

Theseus and the Minotaur—the yearly tribute of seven maidens from Athens—the ancient myths came flooding back into Evans' mind. He was not a born romantic, like Schliemann. He was a scholar. But the evidence seemed overwhelming. There must have been an element of truth in those ancient tales after all. From that moment on, Evans decided to devote the rest of his life not only to excavating Knossos, but to restoring part of it so that future generations would be able to share the vision which he had seen.

During the thirty years in which he worked at Knossos, he spent over 750,000 pounds sterling (more than two million dollars) of his personal fortune on excavating and restoring the Palace, and in producing a great book, *The Palace of Minos*, in which he reconstructed from frescoes, bead-seals (inscribed with pictures), pottery, statues, and the palace buildings—his idea of what this ancient civilization was like. He called it, not Mycenaean, but "Minoan," after King Minos.

# SIX

# THE OLD LEGENDS
# WERE TRUE

In order to make it easier for him to superintend the work, Evans built himself a house near the palace which he called "The Villa Ariadne." Every year, from 1899 to the beginning of the Second World War, he would travel out from England and spend a season at Knossos. Duncan Mackenzie, the faithful, conscientious Scottish excavator, remained with him for many years, keeping, year by year, a careful record of every wall, floor, and layer excavated. Hogarth, after discovering the sacred birth cave of Zeus under Mount Ida, left, but he was replaced by a succession of brilliant archaeologists who worked with Evans.

It should be noticed that Evans, despite his learning and knowledge, always employed experts to help him. For instance, he always employed a resident architect to assist him in reconstructing the palace. This in itself was a tremendous task, because much of the Palace had been built of timber which had decayed, and it was necessary for a skilled architect to decide, from an examination of the column bases and capitals, just how high the columns had stood. Evans never reconstructed anything without being as certain as he could be that what he was reproducing had existed there originally.

Meanwhile, he studied, year by year, the objects brought to light in the palace, and at other Minoan sites in Crete, and prepared notes for his book, *The Palace of Minos,* in which he strove, almost single-handed, to interpret this mysterious Minoan civilization which was much older than that of Mycenae, though the two had much in common. Schliemann had not been able to find the exact dates of the buildings and objects he had found, but Evans was able to establish dates for the main periods of both Minoan and Mycenaean civilization. How did he do this? The answer is not easy to explain unless you are an archaeologist.

Let us put it in this way: Suppose that there was no written history of the United States, and that nobody could date the periods of George Washington, Benjamin Franklin, Abraham Lincoln or John F. Kennedy. But let us imagine that during the periods when these American presidents had governed the United States, certain objects from Europe—such as furniture or pictures, which could be dated in relation to European kings—had been discovered in the ruins of Washington D.C. perhaps two thousand years hence.

Now if, say, a piece of furniture from the reign of King George III of England had been found near objects associated with George Washington, archaeologists would know that Washington lived during the reign of George III, in the latter part of the eighteenth century A.D. Similarly, if a Victorian armchair, dating from about 1850 A.D. had been found in the former home of Abraham Lincoln, it would be safe to assume that Lincoln had been alive at about that time. And if a piece of furniture or a work of art dating from the mid-twentieth century had been discovered in the part of the White House that had been occupied by John F. Kennedy, scholars of the future would be right in thinking that John F. Kennedy had lived in Washington at about that time. The dates would only be approximate, of course.

This was the method which Evans applied, not only to Knossos, but to other Cretan sites and those on the Greek mainland. Instead of European furniture and works of art, he used Ancient Egyptian objects such as miniature statues which bore the names of Ancient Egyptian pharaohs.

For the Ancient Egyptians had a habit of putting the names of their pharaohs on objects of value. Some of these were traded to Crete at various times from about 2000 B.C. onward for 600 years. Egyptologists are able to date these objects fairly accurately, since the Egyptians had a calendar and kept records of the reign dates of their Pharaohs. Thus, if a statuette dating from the reign of the Egyptian Pharaoh, Tuthmosis III, was discovered in a certain layer of the Cretan Palace, Evans could be reasonably certain that the layer dated from between about 1600 and 1550 B.C. And if any Minoan pottery was found in that layer then it, and similar pottery found elsewhere, *even in cities or settlements remote from Knossos,* would also be of approximately the same date. In this way, Evans was able to work out a time scale for the Minoan civilization and was able to establish that the deepest, and therefore oldest, layers at Knossos dated from Neolithic times (that is, from the

New Stone Age, before 3000 B.C.). The highest and latest layers, including most of the buildings lying nearest the surface, dated from about 1400 B.C. at which period the building, and other Cretan palaces, were destroyed.

This is how the scientific archaeologist dates his finds. To him, the *strata,* or levels of an ancient building, are like a "layer cake" except that all the layers of a cake are made at the same time, but the site of an ancient city, which was rebuilt again and again on the old foundations, has layers that may have been built over hundreds of years. The lowest layers are the oldest, the topmost the newest.

Evans could date and explain many of his Cretan finds but there were a number of curious features which puzzled him. For instance, there were what he called *pillar-crypts,* stone-lined chambers in the center of which stood a stone pillar. The pillars were often marked with the sign of the *trident,* the emblem of Poseidon, the God of the Sea. There were also stone-lined pits in the ground which Evans at first thought were baths, as in the case of the pit near the throne room. But again, there were no outlets for water in these pits, and Evans knew that the Minoans knew all about drainage, so the pits were clearly for some other purpose. But what purpose?

There were also what had evidently been religious shrines. One contained a number of beautiful glazed clay statues of a young woman wearing a Minoan Court dress—a tight-waisted, flounced and pleated skirt, and a bolero-type bodice which left the breasts exposed. The statues either held a snake aloft in either hand, or had

Goddess with Snakes (Crete

a snake wreathed around either arm. Evans believed that the statues portrayed the principal deity worshipped by the Minoans. He called her "The Snake Goddess" or "The Mother Goddess," because of her exposed breasts.

There were also colored frescoes depicting other girls and women in court costume, seated in some kind of "grandstand" watching a ceremony. But what ceremony?

Within the Palace, and at other palaces found elsewhere on the island, Evans found flights of steps leading nowhere in particular. These were probably the "grandstands" on which most of the spectators had stood. The ladies, evidently privileged, were seated near the front. The men stood in ranks behind them. It was all very puzzling.

Of one fact Evans was then certain. In his own words he said:

> We know now that the old traditions were true. We have before us a wondrous spectacle—the resurgence, namely, of a civilization twice as old as that of Hellas [ancient, Classical Greece]. It is true that on the old palace site what we see are only the ruins of ruins, but the whole is still inspired with Minos' spirit of order and organization, and the free and natural art of the great architect, Daedalus . . .

Yet still he had not deciphered the writing. Nor had he any written proof that either Minos or Daedalus had ever existed.

# SEVEN

# EUROPE'S
# OLDEST CIVILIZATION

Let us first get clear in our minds what we mean by *civilization*. It does not necessarily mean modern plumbing, beautiful homes, fine buildings and paved streets, though the Minoans had all of these. Nor does it necessarily mean humane behavior. Some of the most civilized epochs, for example, that of the Italian Renaissance, were also viciously cruel times. It means, briefly, a state of society in which large numbers of human beings live an ordered, regulated existence in one area, subject to laws and government, and produce sufficient food to support a class of non-producers—that is, people such as governors, civil servants, artists, craftsmen, thinkers and planners, people freed from the need to wander and hunt for their food and therefore able to settle in one place.

Such civilizations existed in very ancient times in Egypt and the Middle East, as early as 3000 B.C. But until Schliemann and Evans made their discoveries, it was believed that the earliest civilization in Europe was that of Classical Greece, the Greece of Athens, the Parthenon, and the great writers and philosophers who flourished roughly between 700 and 300 B.C. But now it was quite certain that there had been a much earlier civilization in Europe, born on the island of Crete and later copied by the Mycenaeans on the Greek mainland. I say "copied" because, thanks to the dating system or time scale developed by Evans and others, we now know that the Mycenaeans were a different people from the Minoans. We know that they entered Greece about 1900 B.C., when Cretan civilization had already existed for more than 500 years. They came in contact with the Minoans, probably through trade, and imitated their art and culture. But the two peoples were separate and distinct. Mycenae and other mainland cities were not, as was once assumed, Cretan colonies. For instance, the scenes inlaid in gold on Mycenaean daggers are Cretan in style, and may have been produced by Cretan artists. But the scenes themselves, of war and hunting, are not Cretan. The Mycenaeans were a warrior race who lived in fortified castles. The Minoans were a peaceful folk, adequately protected by the sea which surrounded them, with no fear of foreign invasion and no need for fortifications.

The famous *shaft-graves* of Mycenae, where Schliemann found the nineteen bodies richly adorned with gold, can now be dated between 1600 and 1500 B.C., long before the Trojan War, but much later than the earliest Minoan palaces. The Mycenaeans also had colored frescoes painted on their palace walls. Fragments have been found at Tiryns and elsewhere, but, again, these were mainly of hunting scenes. The Mycenaeans also adopted the Minoan writing system, or one of them

Terracotta Bathtub (Crete

—Evans' famous "Linear B." Baked-clay tablets like those found at Knossos have been discovered by the American Professor Carl Blegen at Pylos, a Mycenaean palace, in Greece, and by the Englishman, Professor Alan Wace, at Mycenae. They seem to be identical to the tablets found at Knossos, which Evans dated to about 1400 B.C., when the palace was destroyed.

Because Crete was isolated for so long, and not subject, as Egypt and other civilizations were, to foreign attack, we can trace its development clearly from sites excavated, not only at Knossos, but elsewhere in the island. Many scholars of varying nationalities have helped to discover and interpret these sites. American, Italian and French archaeologists have excavated the Great Palace at Mallia.

It seems that sometime between 4000 and 3000 B.C. the first settlers arrived, probably mainly from Asia though some may have come from Egypt. They were a stone-tool-making people (Neolithic) and were farmers and herdsmen. They settled at first on the plain of Messara, on the eastern tip of Crete, and lived in cave-shelters, where they also buried their dead. Later, fresh immigrants arrived, this time people who knew the art of making bronze tools and weapons. This would have been between about 3000 and 2500 B.C., at a time when this craft was already known in Asia and Egypt.

Now it was possible for the Minoans to make saws and axes to cut down trees, to shape stone in smooth blocks, and to build much finer houses. But these were always reinforced with timber framing, for a reason which will appear later. In about 2000 B.C. it seems that power had been concentrated in three places. At

Knossos, Phaestos (on the south coast), and at Mallia. And here the Minoans began to build great palaces for their rulers. Remember the tradition that Minos had three sons who governed the island?

When we say "palace" we must not confuse these Minoan buildings with mere royal residences. True, the rulers lived there and had magnificent rooms. But within these huge labyrinthine buildings there were also religious shrines (not temples), workshops for carpenters, stonemasons, metalworkers and others, offices for the scribes and record-keepers (including, no doubt, tax-collectors), and the great magazines or storerooms such as those which Evans unearthed at Knossos. In those days, wealth was *in kind*. There was no system of coinage. The wealth of a ruler was reckoned in cattle and crops, including such products as olive oil, wine and wheat. A monarch's wealth could also be judged by the work of his craftsmen. Their pottery and metalwork could be exported in exchange for raw materials not obtainable in Crete. The copper and tin used for making bronze certainly came from overseas, as did the gold. The "Keftiu" depicted on the walls of Ancient Egyptian tombs were traders, or perhaps what we would call "trade representatives" or "commercial travelers" carrying specimens of their trade goods.

The first Cretan palaces were built in about 2000 B.C. but were rebuilt on several later occasions. Archaeologists discovered that on each of these occasions there had been severe earthquakes. They also believe that the reason why the Minoans reinforced their stone buildings with wooden framing was to give them flexibility

43

during the earth tremors which frequently shook the island.

So Minoan civilization progressed from age to age. Its fleet commanded the Aegean Sea (named after Aegeus, father of Theseus). Its merchants carried their goods far and wide, and the country grew rich and prosperous. And then, apparently in about 1400 B.C., all the palaces were destroyed at about the same time. At each site there was evidence of fire and looting. Why there was fire and who the looters were is still not certain. But there are clues, as we shall see.

# EIGHT

# THE BULL
# BENEATH THE EARTH

I said earlier that there were several clues to Minoan civilization in the ancient Greek legends. There is the story of Poseidon, the "Earth-Shaker," who, according to Homer, delighted in bulls; the story of the architect Daedalus who built the Labyrinth, and the story of Europa, who was carried to Crete by Zeus in the form of a bull. Other clues are contained in the story of Ariadne's thread, and the seven noble youths and maidens who were sent each year to be sacrificed to the Minotaur.

Do you know what a *palimpsest* is? In the Middle Ages, when parchment was rare and precious, scribes sometimes wrote on the same sheet of parchment several times. They erased the old writing before adding the new. But often the old writing was still visible underneath. Ancient myths are rather like that. They change and are modified from century to century, but sometimes the original version of the story can still be detected.

The retelling of ancient myths also reminds me of a

party game which I used to play when I was a boy. My friends and I formed a line and everyone in the line had to whisper the story he heard from his neighbor to the next person in line. By the time the story had reached the person at the bottom of the line it had usually been completely changed. The same thing happened to the ancient myths.

Take the legends surrounding Crete. There was no bull-monster, or Minotaur, nor was there a labyrinth beneath the palace. But there was some form of sport, perhaps connected with Minoan religion, in which young athletes, male and female, took part, and this involved leaping over the back of a charging bull, a highly dangerous feat. There is even a *rhyton,* or ritual vase, in the Herakleion Museum showing an unhappy athlete who missed his footing and was gored by the bull. So some element of risk or sacrifice was involved. As for the labyrinth—the palace itself, as we see it today, with its maze of corridors and small rooms, is a labyrinth, and must have appeared so to the Greeks of classical times when they saw Knossos in partial ruin. They themselves, remember, had no buildings of such size and complexity.

As for Daedalus, the great artificer, it is evident that whoever built Knossos was a cunning architect and builder. He understood such features as "light-wells," the shafts running from roof to basement which admit light into "inside" rooms facing the shaft—just as they do in modern hotels, apartment houses and offices. Again, the plumbing system at Knossos could hardly be bettered today, although the palace was built over 3000 years ago. Adjoining the Queen's megaron, or

Bull's Head Rhyton (Crete

main apartment, there is a suite of small rooms including a bathroom and a toilet, which appears to have had some means of flushing the waste away—a "modern" improvement built in 1500 B.C.

In the story of Europa, who came from the coast of Syria and was carried to Crete on a bull's back, we may have inherited a distant memory of the first Minoan settlers who came from Asia, as she did. In each of these stories there is an element of historical truth, but it has become changed and distorted over thousands of years.

Evans himself had vivid personal experience of the awesome power of Poseidon, the Earth-Shaker, in the year 1926, when the great archaeologist was seventy-five. For nearly thirty years he had labored at Knossos, excavating, recording, reconstructing and studying. He had noticed evidence that at several times during the history of the palace there had been severe earthquake shocks which had damaged the structure and necessitated its rebuilding or repair. There was evidence of severe tremors at the other palaces at Mallia and Phaestos.

What happened one warm June night in 1926 is best described in Sir Arthur's own words:

> My own mind . . . was full of past earthquakes and the foreboding of a new convulsion when on June 26, at 9:45 in the evening of a calm, warm day, the shocks began. They caught me reading in bed in a basement room of the headquarters house [the Villa Ariadne, which was of reinforced concrete] and trusting to the exceptional strength of the fabric, I chose to see the earthquake through from

within. [The building] . . . creaked and groaned, and rocked from side to side, as if the whole must collapse. Small objects were thrown about, and a pail, full of water, was splashed nearly empty . . . A dull sound rose from the earth, *like the muffled roar of an angry bull;* our single bell rang, while through the open window came the more distant jangling of the chimes of Herakleion Cathedral, the belfry and dome of which were much damaged. As the quickly repeated shocks produced their cumulative effect, the crashing of roofs made themselves audible, mingled with women's shrieks of terror . . . Meanwhile a mist of dust, lifted upwards by the sudden draught of air, rose sky high, so as almost entirely to eclipse the full moon . . .

Notice now, in Evans' next words, the man of science and the man of imagination speak with one voice. All truly great archaeologists have had this quality of imagination, without which they could not interpret the finds they have made. Sir Arthur continues:

It is something to have heard with one's own ears the bellowing of the bull beneath the earth who, according to primitive belief, tosses it on his horns. It was doubtless the constant need of protection against these petulant bursts of the infernal powers that explains the Minoan tendency to concentrate their worship on . . . their great goddess, wreathed in serpents as Lady of the Underworld [the snake is an emblem of the earth]. Certain structural features, moreover, peculiar to the old Cretan cult suggest the same explanation. Such were the "lustral basins" which were not made for the purpose of holding water, but to which votaries [worshippers] descended for some ritual function that seems to

connect itself with Mother Earth. Such, too, were
the "pillar crypts," windowless, and only lit by arti-
ficial light, the massive central piers which . . .
were provided with vats beside them to receive the
blood of sacrifice.

Evans died in 1941, full of years and honor at the
age of ninety. He left two monuments by which he
will always be remembered—his great, many-volumed
book, *The Palace of Minos*, the fruit of a lifetime's
study of Minoan civilization; and the great Palace of
Knossos itself, which but for his labors and those of his
associates, would today be a mere heap of rubble. It is
one of the wonders of the world, and in the next chap-
ter we shall visit it.

# NINE

# A VISIT TO CRETE

When you arrive on the island of Crete, you step into a land of myth and legend. Whether you come by air or sea, you will certainly come first to Herakleion. As you approach Crete, you will see first the little low island called *Dia,* named after a sea-nymph who angered Hera, Zeus's wife and was turned into a sea monster—which the island of Dia resembles when it is seen from Herakleion. As you land you will see Mount Jukta rising high above you to the south. It is here that the tomb of Zeus allegedly lies. Viewed from certain angles it looks very like the head of a bearded man lying prone.

The Cretans' references to the alleged tomb of Zeus helps explain why, in ancient times, the Greeks used to say, "All Cretans are liars." To the Greeks, Zeus, the king of all the Gods, was immortal; he could not die. Therefore, how could he possibly have a tomb? So the Cretans *were* liars! Here is yet another example of "the myth behind the myth." The Ancient Greeks of classical times were descended from a people called the Dorians, who entered Greece about 1000 B.C. and who worshiped a sky-god called Zeus. But the Minoans, who had been living in Crete for at least 2000 years before the Dorians arrived, probably worshiped a female deity, a mother-goddess whose religion was widespread throughout the Mediterranean and in western Asia. Traditions have it that the queen, who was chief priestess of the goddess, took a new husband for one year only, after which he ceased to be king and was killed. It is possible, though by no means certain, that the so-called "Tomb of Zeus" recalls this far-distant custom, which was abolished when the Greeks occupied Crete. The Minoans probably tried to both accept and then dispose of the rival god Zeus, worshiped by the Greeks. They married him to their Queen, chief priestess of their "Earth Goddess," thus for a time making him part of their own religion. But, by tradition, he could only be king for a year. At the end of that time he would be killed. The "Tomb of Zeus" is his possible, traditional grave.

If you drive through Herakleion by bus, a rather shabby little town, you will see only a few fine Venetian monuments to recommend it. Now you take the road which climbs southward to Knossos. Your bus stops and you climb out. Still, there is nothing remarkable to see. Just a handful of houses; a *taverna* or inn, with a few rickety tables set on the pavement; some olive groves and pale green vineyards. Then you walk through a gate, pass between a shady avenue of trees and suddenly you are in the sunlight, standing in a large paved courtyard beyond which rise dazzling buildings of creamy white stone. You see tapering terracotta-colored pillars, narrow at the bottom and wider at the top, which stand out vividly against limestone walls. The walls are set in a framework of what at first appears to be yellow timber, but which is actually concrete, colored to imitate wood. The wood had decayed or been burned, but Evans had it replaced with these imitation beams so that you could see exactly how the building looked in Minoan times.

Evans' bronze bust looks down at you from its plinth, or pedestal, in the courtyard—a fine, sensitive face with an intellectual forehead and a firm mouth. Evans has been criticized by unthinking people for his reconstructions but it must always be remembered that as the palace was built on, and into, the side of a hill the original timber pillars had burned or decayed and the roofs and ceilings had collapsed and spilled down the hillside. If Evans had not spent so much time, love and money on reconstructing parts (not the whole) of this immense building, there would be nothing for you to see but stones and rubble choked in grass and weeds—which was how Knossos looked when Evans found it over sixty years ago.

Entering by way of the southwest *portico,* or door, the full glory of Knossos strikes you. Blue sky, a green ravine sloping away to your right, and at your back a valley winding into the distant mountains. And in front of you such a bedazzlement of beauty and wonder that you hardly know where to look first. On your left, against the wall of the southwest portico, noble youths with brown skins, dark, curling hair and slim waists, move in procession against a blue background, carrying tall conical rhytons or offering vessels. Origi-

nally, the whole of this and the adjoining corridors were covered with these figures.

Move a few steps eastward, towards the ravine, and you see a reproduction of one of the finest specimens of Minoan art ever found (the original is in the Herakleion Museum). Evans called it "The Prince with the Lily-Crown." You see a young man, with the same lithe muscular body as those of the cupbearers, wearing a huge headdress incorporating lily-flowers. He, too, is one of a number of such youths marching in procession—toward what, or whom? We do not know, since the rest of the frescoes have disappeared.

Such was the scene which greeted the emissaries from Egypt and other foreign powers when they entered the portals of King Minos. They saw what you can see, a broad flight of shallow stone steps leading to a great central courtyard, which originally was surrounded by high buildings. One of these buildings survives, the mysterious throne room, still with that original stone throne in the center of the north wall, bordered by stone benches upon which, presumably, the principal officers of the king (if Knossos was ruled by a king) sat, some 3000 years ago. And facing the throne, lit from above by soft light filtering down from the "light well" enclosed by the buildings, is one of those "lustral pits" which Evans described, approached by a flight of steps. Down those steps the priests of the principal Minoan deity—almost certainly the Snake-Goddess—moved when performing some ceremony of propitiation or offering to the Earth-Mother.

Nearby are workshops, in one of which you can still see, lying on the ground, a piece of stone half-cut

rrup-cup (Candia Museum, Crete)

through, as if its workman had had to abandon his work hurriedly. Not far away are offices in which labored the clerks and scribes who kept records of Minos' wealth on the baked-clay tablets which Evans found but could not decipher. Adjoining them are the long rectangular storerooms, the first part of the palace which Evans discovered, still with the oil jars standing within them, stained with the marks of fire.

On the opposite (eastern) side of the Great Court a noble staircase leads you down by successive flights to the royal apartments. The terra-cotta-colored columns which border it are reconstructions, but the column bases and capitals are original. When Evans found this staircase, most of which is original Minoan work, 3000 years old, he had to employ miners to tunnel down through the debris and shore up the collapsed floors. Only then could his architect safely descend and decide what had been the height and breadth of the columns before ordering their accurate reconstruction. Pieces of charred wood from the original columns still lay in the column bases, further evidence that parts of the palace had been destroyed by fire.

Reaching the foot of the staircase, you enter a suite of beautiful rooms. In one there are remains of the throne, bordered by huge shields of the same "figure-of-eight" pattern which Schliemann observed on the Mycenaean daggers. In another, which Evans called "The Queen's Megaron," dancing girls in long flounced skirts are displayed on the columns, and on the wall dolphins and other sea creatures sport against a blue background. It was near this room that Evans found the bathroom and toilet described before.

If you cross the mountains to the south you will find another equally beautiful palace excavated by the Italian archaeologist Frederico Halbherr and his successors. At Gournia you will be shown a complete Minoan town, excavated originally by the American school of archaeologists, which was apparently occupied mainly by craftsmen. A complete set of carpenters' tools was found in one house, which again appears to have been hurriedly abandoned. And at Mallia there is a third palace of similar type, excavated by the French school of archaeologists. Its staircases, and storage rooms with the wine and oil jars are still intact, as are the remains of the principal megaron.

Wherever you drive through this enchanted island, you will be aware of the long-dead past. By comparison with these Minoan buildings, which existed when Ancient Egypt was in her prime, the works of the later Greeks and Romans seem but of yesterday.

# TEN

# WHY DID IT END?

Evans believed that the Palace of Knossos, and other Minoan royal and princely dwellings, were destroyed at the same time—about 1400 B.C.

At Knossos, Phaestos, and other sites, there are unmistakable marks of destruction by fire. After this final catastrophe, the Minoan civilization never recovered, although at Knossos certain rooms appear to have been occupied by "squatters" up to around 1200 B.C.

Several theories have been put forward to account for the fatal fire. John Pendlebury, Evans' last assistant at Knossos, believed that it was caused, not by an earthquake, but by armed attack, probably by the Mycenaeans from the mainland.

He points out that the throne room shows evidence of hurried preparations for some final act of sacrifice. Ritual jars were overturned, and all the archaeological evidence suggests that, at the last moment in the life of the palace, perhaps when it was already aflame, the Chief Priest or Priestess had been conducting some ceremony in the vain hope of saving the people.

Ceremonial Axe (Crete

Or was it an earthquake that destroyed the Cretan cities? Pendlebury thought not. He pointed out that in ancient times earthquakes did not necessarily cause fires, as they do in modern cities with their electricity and gas mains. No, he said, the destruction of Knossos and the other cities must have been caused by invaders who deliberately set them on fire. And he adds, "There is a name which is always associated with the sack of Knossos . . . *Theseus*. Names have a habit of being remembered long after the deeds with which they are associated are forgotten or garbled . . . And in the last decade of the fifteenth century B.C., on a spring day, when a strong south wind was blowing (Pendlebury deduced this from the direction of the oil stains in the main magazines) which carried the flames of the burning beams horizontally northward, Knossos fell. . . ."

It is a romantic theory and maybe it is true. We don't know. But there is another theory advanced by the Greek Professor Marinatos, which has a number of followers. Marinatos has delved deeply into the question of the destruction of the Minoan Palaces, and has observed that at some time between the sixteenth and fifteenth centuries B.C. (the date cannot be firmly fixed yet) an island called *Santorin*, originally named *Thera*, literally "blew its top." In a titanic volcanic explosion some thirty-three square miles of Santorin were blown into the air or sunk beneath the sea. In fact, when you visit what is left of Santorin today, your ship anchors in a bay made from the submerged crater of the volcano.

In 1883 A.D. the Pacific island of Krakatoa blew up. The force of the explosion was sufficient to cause tidal waves a hundred feet high which swept over the coast of Sumatra and flung quite a large steamer miles inland. Railroad tracks were also swept away, and over 36,000 people died. Yet the crater of Krakatoa is only one third the size of that of Santorin, and, since the depth of the sea between Crete and Santorin is more than one mile deep, the tidal waves, which would have reached the shores of Crete in half an hour could have been of sufficient force, combined with an earthquake, to destroy the palaces of Knossos, Mallia and Phaestos, besides the ports and harbors and the Minoan fleet. Even today you can still see the remains of these harbors deep beneath the water, since, at the time of this catastrophe, the whole island tilted.

My personal belief is that the disaster was caused by an exceptionally violent earthquake, probably accompanied by tidal waves, and that the Mycenaeans of the mainland subsequently exploited the misfortune of the Minoans, occupying the island and founding a new dynasty of Greek-speaking kings who ruled from Knossos.

# ELEVEN

# ARIADNE'S THREAD

Early in this book I said that following the complexities of archaeological discovery in Greece and Crete was as difficult as Theseus' task of finding his way through the Labyrinth. The story, as told so far, may appear simple. Indeed, I hope it does. But in fact it is not simple at all, and many important questions remain unanswered to this day.

All we can be certain of is this: *That the earliest civilization in Europe began in Crete in about 3000 B.C. or a little later, and that between 1900 and 1600 B.C. a new people whom we call "Mycenaean" for convenience, entered Greece and came to rule over it.* Where they came from we cannot be certain, but they certainly spoke a primitive form of Greek. Therefore, they can claim to be the first Greeks to enter Greece. What name they gave themselves is not known (the word "Greece" comes from Roman historians), but it is possible that they were the much-feared "bronze-clad Achaeans" described by Homer as having besieged and sacked Troy.

From an examination of their earliest graves, it seems clear that the first Myceneans were at a low level of civilization. Their "grave goods" (objects buried in their tombs) were poor and paltry. Yet, in about 1600 B.C. their princes and princesses were being buried with great pomp at Mycenae. Their bodies were surrounded by wonderful objects of gold, silver and bronze so like those of Crete that we have no doubt that these objects were either made by Cretan workmen or by Mycenaean craftsmen trained by Cretans.

In brief, the "Mycenaeans" or Achaeans must have come into contact with the more highly-developed civilization of Crete, and copied it. The old theory, advanced by Evans, that Mycenean cities were merely Cretan colonies, no longer holds water. The two peoples were quite distinct and separate in character, the Mycenaeans being warlike and predatory, while the Cretans were pacific.

The pottery, art, tools, weapons and architecture of the two peoples were generally similar, but if you study them carefully, for example in the Archaeological Museum in Athens, you will see that there are distinct differences. Again you can see that the Mycenaeans lived in strong-walled cities in Greece such as Mycenae, Tiryns and Pylos while the Minoans, or Cretans, lived peaceably in unfortified towns, relying on their fleet for protection, as Thucydides has said. The Minoans commanded the sea and traded widely throughout the Mediterranean, selling their goods in Asia, Egypt and the Aegean Islands.

Then there came a time, though the date is still uncertain, when Crete fell, and the Mycenaeans took

over. From that period onward it was the Mycenaeans, and not the Minoans, who ruled the East Mediterranean and commanded the trade. Typical Mycenaean pottery and other goods are found in many places, from coastal Syria to Sicily and North Africa. The Minoans, who had founded civilization in Europe, simply disappeared from the picture.

This theory, that the Mycenaeans conquered the Minoans and inherited their Empire, had been advanced by a number of people, notably Professor Carl Blegen of Cincinatti University, and Professor Alan Wace of England. Evans opposed it, but confirming evidence came in 1953 when a young English architect, Michael Ventris, announced that, with the help of British and American collaborators, he had succeeded, after seventeen years of effort, in deciphering the "Linear B" writing system—a task to which he had applied himself, ever since, as a schoolboy, he had heard Sir Arthur Evans lecture on the subject.

I had the great good fortune to know Ventris personally. He was about thirty-three when I first knew him: a handsome, modest Englishman who had already made a great career for himself as an architect. Deciphering "Linear B" was to him just a hobby and I was once told that when he was a navigator in the Royal Air Force Bomber Command, he used to work on the decipherment on his map table. His success was hailed in the press as "the Everest of Greek Archaeology," as indeed it was, particularly as Ventris did not have what is called a "bilingual clue," an inscription of the same words in two different languages, one known and the other unknown.

Teapot Jar" (Candia Museum, Crete)

He died, tragically, at the very moment of his triumph, in a motor accident, at the age of thirty-four. A famous Greek poet, Menander, who lived some 2,200 years ago, wrote the well-known lines, "Those whom the Gods love die young," which apply exactly to Michael Ventris. The language which Evans had striven, unavailingly, to decipher, turned out to be an early form of Greek. And as it was found at Mycenae, Pylos, and also at Knossos, the theory is that before 1400 B.C. the Mycenaeans had already established themselves in Crete.

Schliemann's Mycenaeans were, in fact, the first Greek-speaking people to enter Greece, nearly a thousand years before the Dorians, who were the ancestors of the classical Greeks, with whom we are most familiar. The other script, which Evans called "Linear A" was probably that of the Minoans, which the Greeks adapted. But it has yet to be deciphered.

I am glad to say that this story is not yet complete. Evans could have been wrong in some of his theories, for example that Knossos fell in 1400 B.C. Again, it is still not certain how the Minoan civilization came to an end. Moreover, the little tablets, from which scholars expected so much, turned out to be mere lists or inventories of palace stores kept by the Mycenaean scribes: so many head of cattle, so many chariots, so many slaves, etc. with details of allotments of land, and offerings reserved for the Gods. It is interesting to find such names as Zeus, Hera, Poseidon (at this period apparently more important than Zeus) and Artemis mentioned, besides the names of such Homeric heroes as Hector.

But to the general reader, as distinct from the archaeologist, the tablets are disappointing. It is almost as if, three thousand years hence, someone had heard of a great poet named Shakespeare, and the only writing of his they could find was his laundry list.

Perhaps, who knows, some day a reader of this book may find a document in "Linear B" or "Linear A" which tells the true, original story of the Trojan War. Much remains to be done, and sometime there will be a future Schliemann, or an Evans, to pick up the torch of learning, and to carry it forward again in Crete.

# INDEX

70